Copilot's Ultimate Guidebook

Empowering Individuals and Businesses for Peak Performance

Matthew H. Larsen

Copyright

About the Author

Matthew H. Larsen is a famous person in the worlds of technology and innovation. He is praised for his deep insights and valuable contributions to the tech community. Matthew has become a major voice in the field of artificial intelligence and how it can be used in both personal and professional settings. He has a background that is both academically and practically strong.

Larsen went to MIT and got a degree in computer science. He then went to Stanford University and got a Ph.D. in artificial intelligence. His academic journey set him up for a career full of new ideas and research. With Matthew, you can learn a lot of different things, like machine learning, software development, and how to use AI in business.

Before writing "Copilot's Ultimate Guidebook: Empowering Individuals and Businesses for Peak Performance," Larsen worked in Silicon Valley for more than ten years on a number of innovative projects. His main goal was to make more people able to use and acquire advanced technologies. His desire to make technology more accessible led him to create training programmes and workshops that help people and business teams use AI tools like Copilot.

Matthew is more than just an author and tech expert. He has taught courses at several top universities and has been a keynote speaker at numerous technology conferences around the world. His ability to translate complex technological concepts into understandable and actionable insights has made him a sought-after consultant for top tech businesses.

In his free time, Larsen is an avid coder and likes contributing to open-source projects. He believes in the power of community-driven development and is an advocate for good AI practices. His book, "Copilot's Ultimate Guidebook," is a reflection of his commitment to empowering people with the knowledge and tools they need to succeed in the rapidly changing digital world.

Table of content

Appendices

A: Quick Reference Guide

B: Glossary of Terms

C: Additional Resources and Reading

Introduction

Understanding Copilot

In today's rapidly changing technological environment, Copilot stands out as a groundbreaking tool, designed to revolutionize the way individuals and businesses interact with digital technology. At its core, Copilot is an advanced artificial intelligence system that offers intuitive help, enhances productivity, and fosters innovation across various platforms and industries. This intelligent assistant is not just about executing tasks; it's about knowing the nuanced needs of its users and adapting to those needs in real-time.

The essence of Copilot lies in its ability to learn from exchanges, making it more than just a software tool - it's a learning and evolving partner. Whether you're a software developer looking to streamline your coding process, a business professional seeking to automate routine tasks, or an individual exploring the realms of AI, Copilot is meant to help you in achieving your goals with greater efficiency and accuracy.

How This Guidebook Will Help You

"Copilot's Ultimate Guidebook:
Empowering Individuals and Businesses for Peak Performance"** is designed to be your comprehensive resource in understanding and utilizing Copilot to its best potential.

This reference serves multiple purposes:

1. **Educational Resource**: It breaks down the complexities of Copilot, making its advanced technologies approachable and understood to all users, regardless of their technical background.

2. **Practical Manual**: The guidebook provides step-by-step instructions, tips, and best practices for utilizing Copilot in various situations. From basic setup to advanced customization, it covers all aspects to ensure you can use Copilot successfully.

3. **Inspirational Companion**: Through real-world examples, case studies, and success stories, this guidebook will inspire you to explore new ways to use Copilot,

pushing the limits of what you thought was possible in your personal and professional life.

4. **Future Outlook**: As the landscape of AI continues to evolve, this guidebook will help you stay ahead of the curve by giving insights into future developments and how you can prepare for and leverage these changes.

By the end of this guidebook, you'll not only have a complete understanding of Copilot but also be equipped with the knowledge and skills to harness its full potential, leading to enhanced performance, creativity, and innovation in your endeavors.

Chapter 1

The Basics of Copilot

What is Copilot?

Copilot is an advanced artificial intelligence tool that works as a virtual assistant, designed to significantly enhance productivity and efficiency in various tasks. It leverages machine learning and a vast database of information to provide intelligent support to its users. Copilot's primary objective is to simplify complex tasks, automate routine processes, and offer insightful advice, making it an invaluable asset for both individual users and business entities. Its versatility allows it to adapt to a wide range of industries and workflows, making it a universal tool in the world of digital technology.

Key Features and Capabilities

1. **Intuitive User Interface**: Copilot boasts a user-friendly interface that is easy to navigate, ensuring that users can efficiently access its features regardless of their technical knowledge.

2. **Customizable Workflows**: One of Copilot's standout features is its ability to change to the unique workflow of each user. It can be customized to align with specific tasks and preferences, enhancing personal and business productivity.

3. **Advanced Machine Learning Algorithms:** At the heart of Copilot's functions are sophisticated machine learning algorithms. These algorithms allow Copilot to learn from user interactions, continuously improving its assistance over time.

4. **Integration Capabilities**: Copilot seamlessly integrates with a variety of software and platforms, extending its usefulness across different environments.

5. **Real-Time Assistance and Feedback**: Users receive instant assistance and feedback from Copilot, which is crucial for time-sensitive tasks and decision-making processes.

6. **Data Analysis and Insights**: Copilot can analyze large volumes of data, giving valuable insights and recommendations to aid in decision-making.

Setting Up Copilot for First-Time Users

1. **Creating an Account**: The first step is to make a user account with Copilot. This includes providing basic information and setting up login credentials.

2. **Initial Configuration:** After account creation, users are led through an initial setup process. This includes configuring basic settings and preferences to tailor Copilot to the user's unique needs.

3. **Integrating with Other Tools**: Users can integrate Copilot with other apps and tools they use. This step is important for maximizing Copilot's usefulness in streamlining workflows.

4. **Learning the Interface:** Familiarizing oneself with Copilot's interface is important. The guidebook provides a full overview of the interface, along with tips for navigation and usage.

5. **Starting with Basic Tasks**: It's suggested that first-time users start by using Copilot for basic tasks. This gradual approach helps in knowing its functionalities better and gaining confidence in using more advanced features.

6. **Accessing Support and Resources:** Copilot comes with a range of support choices and resources. New users are urged to explore these to enhance their understanding and get the most out of the tool.

This chapter lays the basis for users to begin their journey with Copilot, setting the stage for more advanced topics and usage situations covered in the subsequent chapters.

Chapter 2:

Advanced Features and Customization

Customizing Copilot for Your Needs
Customization is key to realizing the potential of Copilot. This section delves into the various ways you can tailor Copilot to fit your unique requirements and preferences. It covers:

1. Personalized Settings:

Learn how to adjust Copilot's settings to align with your individual workflow and goals. This includes changing interface layouts, notification settings, and more.

2. **Adapting to User Behavior:**

Copilot's ability to adapt to your unique usage habits is one of its most powerful features. Understand how to train Copilot to notice and adjust to your working style and preferences.

3. **Creating Custom Commands and Shortcuts:**

This part teaches you how to create custom commands and shortcuts in Copilot, allowing quicker and more efficient task execution.

Advanced Tools and Techniques

This section explores the more sophisticated aspects of Copilot, giving insights into how to leverage its full capabilities:

1. Deep Dive into AI Capabilities:

Get a detailed understanding of the advanced AI algorithms that power Copilot, and how they can be utilized for complex jobs and problem-solving.

2. Automating Complex Workflows:

Learn how to use Copilot to automate intricate and time-consuming workflows, greatly boosting efficiency and productivity.

3. **Data Analysis and Visualization Tools:** Discover how to use Copilot for in-depth data analysis and building insightful visualizations, aiding in better decision-making.

Integrating with Other Software and Platforms

Integration is important for a seamless experience. This part guides you through the process of integrating Copilot with other software and platforms:

1. **Compatibility and Integration Guides:** Detailed advice on how to integrate Copilot with popular software tools and platforms,

ensuring smooth operation within your existing ecosystem.

API Integration: For users with programming knowledge, this part covers how to use Copilot's API to build custom integrations and functionalities.

2. Collaboration Features:

Learn about Copilot's tools that support collaborative work environments, including shared workflows and team project management.

3. Security and Compliance:

Understand the security measures and compliance processes involved in integrating Copilot with other systems, ensuring your data remains safe and protected.

By the end of this chapter, users will have a thorough understanding of how to customize and integrate Copilot into their workflows, harnessing its advanced features for enhanced productivity and efficiency in various complex scenarios.

Chapter 3

Copilot for Individuals

Enhancing Personal Productivity
This part addresses how individuals can use Copilot to boost their daily productivity. Key areas include:

1. **Task Management**: Learn how to use Copilot for organizing and managing daily tasks, setting reminders, and tracking progress to improve efficiency in personal projects and everyday activities.

2. **Learning and Skill Development:** Discover how Copilot can help in personal learning journeys, whether it's acquiring a

new skill, language learning, or pursuing a hobby.

3. **Health and Wellness Tracking:** Understand how to leverage Copilot for health and wellness goals, including fitness tracking, food planning, and mental health monitoring.

Creative Uses of Copilot in Everyday Life

This section discusses innovative and unconventional ways to incorporate Copilot into everyday life:

1. **Home Automation**: Tips on integrating Copilot with smart home devices to make an interconnected and automated living space.

2. **Financial Management**: Guidance on using Copilot for personal finance management, planning, and investment tracking.

3. **Journey Planning**: Discover how Copilot can be a journey companion, aiding in itinerary planning, language translation, and cultural insights.

Case Studies: Personal Success Stories

Real-life stories and testimonials provide clear examples of how Copilot has transformed the lives of individuals:

1. **The Busy Professional:** A case study of a professional who used Copilot to balance work and personal life, efficiently managing time and chores.

2. **The Lifelong Learner**: This story shows an individual who utilized Copilot as a tool for continuous learning and skill development.

3. **The Health Enthusiast:** A narrative showcasing how someone incorporated Copilot into their fitness and health practice, achieving remarkable wellness goals.

Each case study will provide insights into the specific challenges faced by these people and how they leveraged Copilot to overcome these challenges, offering readers relatable situations and practical applications of Copilot in various aspects of personal life.

Chapter 4

Copilot in the Business Environment

Implementing Copilot in Your Business
This section offers a comprehensive guide
for businesses to integrate Copilot into their
operations effectively. It covers:

1. **Assessment and Planning:**
Steps to evaluate your business goals and
plan the integration of Copilot accordingly.
This includes identifying key places where
Copilot can add value.

2. **Customization for Business Needs:**
Tailoring Copilot to meet unique business
requirements, such as automating business

processes, data management, and customer relationship management.

3. Training and Adoption:

Strategies for training employees on using Copilot and encouraging its adoption throughout the company to maximize its benefits.

4. Scaling with Copilot:

Insights on how to scale the use of Copilot as your business grows, ensuring the tool changes with your company's needs.

Case Studies: Businesses Transforming with Copilot

This section shows real-world examples of businesses that have successfully integrated Copilot into their operations:

1 **The Startup Story**:
A case study of a startup that used Copilot to streamline its processes, improve productivity, and drive innovation.

2 **The Corporate Transformation:**
An exploration of how a large company implemented Copilot to enhance efficiency, reduce costs, and promote a culture of continuous improvement.

3 **The Small Business Success**:

A narrative focusing on a small business that leveraged Copilot to manage resources better, improve customer service, and compete in the market successfully.

Collaborative Features and Team Management

In this part, the attention is on how Copilot facilitates teamwork and collaboration:

1 **Team cooperation Tools:**

An overview of Copilot's features that support team cooperation, such as shared workspaces, project management tools, and communication integrations.

2 **Managing Teams with Copilot**:

Guidance on using Copilot for team management, including job delegation, progress tracking, and performance analytics.

3 **Enhancing Remote Work:**

Tips on leveraging Copilot to support and improve remote work environments, ensuring team cohesion and productivity irrespective of location.

By the end of this chapter, businesses will have a clear understanding of how to adopt, use, and benefit from Copilot in their operations, with practical examples and tips for optimizing team collaboration and management.

Chapter 5

Navigating Challenges and Troubleshooting

Common Issues and Their Solutions

This guidebook addresses typical challenges users might face while using Copilot and provides practical solutions:

1 Technical Glitches:

Covers common technical issues like software bugs, integration problems, or speed lags, and offers step-by-step solutions.

2 User Interface Navigation:

Helps users who may struggle with navigating Copilot's interface, giving tips and tricks to improve user experience.

3 Customization Difficulties:
Provides solutions for users having challenges in customizing Copilot to their specific needs, including how to reset settings and start the customization process afresh.

Tips for Effective Troubleshooting

This part offers general tips and methodologies for troubleshooting problems with Copilot:

1 Diagnostic Tools:
An overview of built-in diagnostic tools in Copilot and how to use them to find and resolve issues.

2 Problem-Solving Strategies:

Teaches problem-solving strategies such as breaking down complex problems into smaller parts, using process of elimination, and keeping detailed records of changes and outcomes.

3 Maintaining Copilot:

Guidance on regular maintenance practices for Copilot, like software updates and data backups, to avoid potential issues.

Seeking Support and Resources

For times when self-troubleshooting is not enough, this part guides users on how to seek further help:

1 **Using the Copilot Help Center:**
Instructions on how to navigate the Copilot Help Center for articles, FAQs, and tips.

2 **Community Support:**
Information on how to leverage the Copilot user community for help, including forums and online groups.

3 **Professional Support Services:**
Details on how to contact Copilot's professional support team for technical help,

including contact information and what to expect during the support process.

By the end of this chapter, users will be equipped with the knowledge and resources to effectively handle any challenges.

Chapter 6

The Future of Copilot

Upcoming Features and Updates

In this part, the guidebook discusses anticipated developments and enhancements in future versions of Copilot:

1 Roadmap Preview:

Provides a sneak peek into the planned updates and new features that are on the horizon for Copilot, giving users a glimpse of what to expect in terms of functionality and user experience.

2 Innovative Features on the Anvil:

Discusses cutting-edge features currently in development, such as more advanced AI powers, enhanced integration choices, and more intuitive user interfaces.

3 Constant Improvement Process:

Explains the process behind how user feedback and technological advancements drive the constant improvement and evolution of Copilot.

The Evolving Role of Copilot in Technology

This part delves into the broader effect and growing significance of Copilot in the tech industry:

1 **Trends and Predictions:**
Examines current trends in AI and automation, and predicts how these trends will shape the role of tools like Copilot in the future.

2 **Expanding Application Areas:**
Discusses possible new domains and industries where Copilot could be applied, highlighting its versatility and adaptability.

3 **Ethical Considerations and AI Governance:**
Addresses the ethical implications and governance issues surrounding AI tools like Copilot, stressing the importance of responsible use.

Preparing for Future Advancements

The final part offers guidance on how individuals and businesses can prepare for and adapt to the evolving landscape of Copilot:

1 **Staying Informed and Educated:**
Emphasizes the value of staying updated with the latest developments in Copilot and the wider field of AI and automation.

2 **Skills Development and Training:**
Advises on the types of skills and training that will be helpful for users to fully leverage future versions of Copilot.

3 **Strategic Planning for Businesses:**
Offers insights for businesses on how to strategically plan for integrating future advancements of Copilot into their operations for continued growth and competitiveness.

By the end of this chapter, readers will have a comprehensive understanding of the future trajectory of Copilot and how they can prepare themselves and their groups to make the most of these exciting advancements.

Chapter 7

Building a Community Around Copilot

Engaging with the Copilot User Community

This section highlights the importance of community engagement for Copilot users and offers strategies for effective participation:

1 **Joining the Community**:
Guides readers on how to find and join Copilot user communities, including online boards, social media groups, and local meetups.

2 **Active Participation**:

Encourages active participation in discussions, webinars, and community events, giving tips on how to participate meaningfully and learn from fellow users.

3 **Community Resources:**

Introduces different resources available within the community, such as user-created guides, tutorials, and problem-solving threads.

Sharing Knowledge and Best Practices

This part focuses on the exchange of information and experiences within the Copilot community:

1 **Adding to the Knowledge Base:**
Encourages users to share their own experiences, tips, and best practices with the community, adding to the collective knowledge base.

2 **Learning from Peers:**
Highlights how users can learn from the experiences and ideas of other community members, including case studies, success stories, and creative uses of Copilot.

3 **Mentorship Opportunities:**

Discusses the benefits of both getting and providing mentorship within the Copilot group, fostering a culture of mutual growth and support.

Collaborative Opportunities and Networking

This section delves into the collaborative and networking opportunities offered through the Copilot community:

1 **Collaborative Projects:** Introduces opportunities for users to work on projects with other community members, leveraging diverse skills and perspectives.

2   **Networking Events:** Provides information on networking events, both virtual and in-person, where Copilot users can meet, share ideas, and build professional relationships.

3   **Influencing Future Developments:** Explains how active community members can play a role in influencing the future development of Copilot by giving collective feedback and ideas to the developers.

By the end of this chapter, readers will have a clear understanding of the benefits of engaging with the Copilot user community, the various ways they can share and gain knowledge, and how they can collaborate and network with other users to improve their experience with Copilot.

Conclusion

Key Takeaways from the Guidebook

This final part recaps the most important lessons and insights offered throughout the guidebook:

1 **Understanding Copilot:**
Emphasizes the comprehensive nature of Copilot as an AI tool and its ability to transform both personal and business activities.

2 **Customization and Integration**:
Highlights the value of customizing and integrating Copilot into your unique workflows to maximize its efficiency and effectiveness.

3 **The Power of Community:**

Reiterates the value of interacting with the Copilot user community for knowledge sharing, collaborative opportunities, and continuous learning.

4 **Preparation for the Future:**

Underlines the necessity of staying educated and adaptable to leverage future advancements in Copilot and related technologies.

Your Next Steps with Copilot

This part offers a guide on how to continue after finishing the guidebook:

1 **Setting Up and playing:** Encourages readers to start by setting up Copilot, playing with its features, and customizing it according to their needs.

2 **Engaging with the Community**: Advice on taking active steps to join and participate in the Copilot community for improved learning and networking.

3 **Applying Knowledge**: Motivates readers to apply the knowledge and skills gained

from the guidebook in real-world situations, both personally and professionally.

Continuing Your Journey of Learning and Growth

Importance of ongoing learning and adaptation:

1   **Lifelong Learning**: Emphasizes the concept of lifelong learning, especially in the ever-evolving field of technology, and encourages readers to continually seek new information and skills.

2   **Staying Updated:** Advises on keeping up-to-date with the latest developments in Copilot and the broader AI and technology environment.

3   **Sharing and Reflecting**: Encourages readers to share their experiences and learnings with others, and to think on their own growth and development as they use Copilot.

This conclusion serves as a motivational closing, inspiring readers to not only utilize Copilot to its fullest potential but also to become a part of the evolving journey of AI and technology in order adding to their personal and professional growth.

Appendices

A: Quick Reference Guide

This section serves as a handy tool for users to quickly access key information about Copilot:

Getting Started: A simplified step-by-step guide to setting up and starting with Copilot.

Common Commands and Shortcuts: Lists the most commonly used Copilot commands and keyboard shortcuts for easy reference.

Troubleshooting Checklist: A quick checklist to diagnose and fix common issues experienced by Copilot users.

Contact Information for Support: Essential contact details for Copilot's customer help for quick reference.

B: Glossary of Terms

The glossary gives clear definitions of terms and jargon related to Copilot and AI technology:

Technical Terms: Definitions of technical terms used throughout the guidebook, helping readers understand complex ideas.

Copilot-Specific Jargon: Explains specific terminologies and features unique to Copilot, aiding in better understanding of the guidebook.

General AI and Technology Terms: Covers broader terms in the fields of AI and technology that are important to understanding and using Copilot.

C: Additional Resources and Reading

This section lists extra materials for those interested in further exploring Copilot and related technologies:

Books and Articles: Recommended books, academic papers, and articles for deeper knowledge of AI, machine learning, and their applications.

Online Resources: A compilation of websites, blogs, and forums where readers can find the latest news, tutorials, and talks on Copilot and AI technologies.

Courses and Webinars: Information about relevant online courses, webinars, and workshops for continued learning and skill growth in AI and Copilot usage.

By providing these appendices, the guidebook ensures that readers have quick access to important information, a clear understanding of key terms, and resources for further exploration, making their journey with Copilot as smooth and enriching as possible.